FAMILY MATTERS

In the Beginning...

FAMILY MATTERS

In the Beginning...

Kemi Akindele

©2016 Kemi Akindele.

ISBN: 978-1-365-02293-7

Correspondence:
In Canada:
The Incubator International
P. O. Box 680
St. Paul, Alberta, Canada
T0A 3A0
Tel: +1-780-645-7722
E. Mail: bode@theincubatorintl.org
Website: www.theincubatorintl.org

In Nigeria:
Heritage Multimedia Outreach
8, Adejumo Cresent, Providence Estate,
Sitaga Bus Stop, Eleyele, Ibadan.
Tel: ++234-803-073-2655

All rights reserved. This book is protected by copyright laws. The contents or cover may not be reproduced in whole or in part or in any form for commercial purposes. The use of short quotations or occasional page copying for personal or group study is permitted. Other forms of usage must be with the permission of the author and publisher.

To Jesus Christ, my personal Saviour and Lord
To my nuclear Family, Olabode, Oluwatimileyin and
Oluwatunmise Akindele
To my extended family:
Oluwatomi and Kayode Famade,
Titobiloluwa Akindele and Ilerioluwa Oyedele
And to my late mother, Felicia Omoyeni Bello:
Mom, your good work lives on...

Table of Contents

Acknowledgments ………………………………….... 9

Praise for Family Matters ……………………………. 11

Foreword ……………………………………………........ 13

Introduction ……………………………………………... 15

Chapter 1   My Story……………………………… 21

Chapter 2   What Is A Family? ………………………. 37

Chapter 3   The Old And The New Testament ……… 53

Chapter 4   The Extended Family ……………………... 71

Chapter 5   Children ……………………………….... 79

Chapter 6   Blueprints For An Adult Christian Life … 97

Chapter 7   The Role Of The Family In Setting

            Up New Families ……...…………............... 119

ACKNOWLEDGMENTS

With love and affection, I acknowledge the contributions of my one and only husband, Olabode who right from the beginning of our relationship has been passionate to see me become the best person I could ever be. He pushed me to start writing this book even when I had no title.

To our new found helper but longstanding friend, Olutoyin Oladele, thanks for all your hard work and encouragement.

Our senior friends and brethren, Dr & Dr Mrs Segun and Seyi Oyedele; Dr & Dr Mrs Segun and Funmi Alawale; Dr & Dr Mrs Niyi & Funmi Bankole; Dr & Mrs Yinka & Toyin Dada; Dr & Mrs Femi & Ireti Adetunji; Mr & Mrs Debo Adetunji. Thanks so much for reading the manuscripts and for your suggestions and words of encouragement.

I want to acknowledge our Skype Bible Study team: our children, their cousin, Seyitan Hamid-Oke in Brampton, our dear friends, the Oyedeles (Segun, Seyi, Ileri, Babalolu & Ife) who live in Kelowna, BC, a dear brother who was influential in training our girls in music, Debo Adetunji and his lovely wife, Funke who live in South Africa. From the Caribbean Island, Toyin Alawale; from the UK, Joy

Alawale (nee Troko); from St. Lucia, the family of Dr. Ogunlusi (Gbemi, Akinlolu & Tofunmi); Dr & Mrs Isaac and Felicia Amusan; the family of Dr Adebayo (Francis, Abiola, Gideon & little Francis); and Oluwadunsin Oluwole from St. Paul - all on the Skype meetings.

I also acknowledge the contributions of everyone who has joined for one or two discussions.

Thank you all!

PRAISE FOR
FAMILY MATTERS

God has given Kemi not just a calling to teach His unadulterated Word, but He has also given her a specific message for the transformation of one of the most important God-ordained institutions on earth. Through this book Kemi speaks directly to the heart of the reader with the aim of birthing hope and restoration. As you read, we pray that not only will you receive the message that your family matters to God and to this generation, but you will also enter into a time of real revival and restoration in all that concerns your life and family. Be abundantly blessed.
Drs. Olusegun & Oluseyi Oyedele, Kelowna, BC, Canada

Dr. Kemi Akindele has written from sound Biblical principles, from her wealth of experience which is rich and diverse, and from her strong heart's conviction. Having known her for decades, Kemi is an uncompromising Christian who is very strong on living by unchanging biblical values. This, no doubt, is a very practical book that would offer an invaluable guide to all age groups in various roles but particularly to the young people who have just started their families or intending to commence one. I strongly recommend it to all.
Dr. Ezekiel Olusegun Alawale, The Senior Pastor; God's Vineyard Ministries, Nottingham UK

Kemi has a story to tell. She has succeeded in addressing the old, young adult and the young. Many great thoughts are expressed in this book and I believe the book speaks for itself.

Dr. Olaniyi Bankole, Consultant Surgeon; Mother & Child Hospital, Lagos, Nigeria.

In her characteristic affinity for God's truth, Dr. Kemi Akindele has shown through this book how a godly family should operate in this stressful world. The truths in this book will never stress anyone who embraces and implements all the nuggets therein, but will rather set free. It is an inspiring piece that will bless many generations to come. I strongly recommend this book to everyone who desires a stress free family life.

Dr. Olayinka Dada, Senior Pastor, Restoration House, Hamilton Canada

FOREWORD

I have had unique opportunities to sit and listen to my wife at different times as she shared the insights God gave to her as regards the family institution. Each time, my mind was challenged to check the scriptures again and again. We have subsequently had various discussions and reasoning sessions together, and with our children and our friends.

I have also listened to her speak at Conferences and I have come to acknowledge that Kemi has a God-given message that will lead to the restoration of God's mind for the family.

This book is only a portion of the message in her spirit, and I strongly recommend it to you. I am sure it will challenge your thoughts and tremendously bless your heart. So, dive in and start to glean.

Bode Akindele
President,
The Incubator International, Canada

INTRODUCTION

The word *restoration* recently caught my attention while ruminating over some extended family issues. From the depths of my heart, the phrase 'family restoration' floated out. What does that mean and why should I be thinking of writing a book on an issue that so many have written about?

Several years ago, I wrote a small book titled 'A Letter to My Little Girl' and a dear friend of mine asked why I didn't write one to my little boy. I replied, 'I am female, not male!' He responded, "Paul the apostle was unmarried but he wrote about marriage." I had no other argument.

Why family restoration?

The degree of dysfunctionality in families is appalling. Systems are failing in all nations, divorce rates are climbing, and domestic violence and disruptions are affecting a whole new generation.

To compound matters, there are lots of confusing issues over political correctness versus fruitful living. Many people portrayed by the media as idols and heroes have struggling families. With this degree of dysfunctionality going on, there is a huge need for restoration.

What is Restoration?

Restoration simply means to get a thing back to its original state and where the family is concerned the original structure came from God.

C.S. Lewis once asserted, *'Every problem can be solved if we go back to where we went wrong'*. Sometimes the best way to start doing something right is to stop doing something wrong.

The purpose of this book is to discuss certain issues from a Biblical perspective so that it can lead to a better understanding of family operations. It's important to discuss family matters because family matters.

I will not be using cultural, national nor denominational standards because I believe these are part of the reasons for the troubles we are in.

Believers are spread all over the world from different cultures, races and denominational backgrounds and my purpose is to find common grounds about the family according to the scriptures. What may be culturally or politically correct in Canada may not be in Nigeria, but the

Scripture is always relevant to the believer - irrespective of geographical location.

I will be discussing the Bible for solutions on the basis of 2 Cor. 3:4-6

> **We say this because we have confidence in God through Christ. There is nothing in us that allows us to claim that we are capable of doing this work. The capacity we have comes from God; it is he who made us capable of serving the new covenant, which consists not of a written law but of the Spirit. The written law brings death, but the Spirit gives life. 2 Corinthians 3:4-6 G NT**

This is my first book on family matters and there is much more to come. Even now, I have deliberately decided to leave out some issues for the second in this series. I prefer to make my points in bits and pieces, as I believe it allows for better assimilation of each point which hopefully, will turn into action and achieve positive changes first in our minds and then in our lives.

On this note, I submit this book to your perusal under God, believing it will bless and change you.

...In the beginning, God created family
(Anonymous)

Chapter 1

MY STORY

I am the second of four children born to my parents who were both the first set of graduates from the University of Ife (now Obafemi Awolowo University), Ile-Ife, Nigeria.

We lived mostly with my mother because our parents got officially divorced when I was seven years old. They had never really lived together even before the divorce and I do not remember any day when we all slept together as one family under the same roof.

Mom came from a polygamous family and she was the second of thirteen siblings in all. She had to take care of all her younger siblings at one stage or the other as she graciously handled taking care of the four of us as well. She was a career woman and a brilliant administrator who was also God-fearing and very active in her church.

Understandably, Mom was not a home maker. She hardly ever had the time to get to do domestic activities, so we had house helps who would do everything around the house. At some point we had four house helps plus her official driver who took us around, along with other relatives who were living with us at that time.

Daddy would visit once in a while but he would never come into the house. In fact, he stayed many times at the school gate and we had to visit with him standing by his car in the full glare of curious students who wanted to catch a glimpse of him. This was because Mom was a school principal and we lived in a school compound with the boarding students.

I gained admission into Obafemi Awolowo University (then University of Ife) in 1983. I gave my heart to Jesus early 1984 through the ministry of many brethren from the Evangelical Christian Union (ECU). That was the turning point in my life.

Before then, I had the notion that all men were bad and all women were good. I was out to prove to the world that what a man could do, a woman could do better. Marriage was going to be avoided for as long as possible while I faced a highly ranked career. If and when it did happen, it would be on the premise that I would get even for the injustices my Mom had experienced in her marriage.

But then Jesus came into my heart and things started changing. What I learnt from the Bible was vastly different from what I saw around me.

At this point, I was getting to know the experiences of my friends who also had lots of issues about their family lives. The stories were basically the same. If there was no divorce, there was polygamy or sibling favoritism. With my new world view as a believer, I made up my mind I was going to allow God to make a difference with my marriage.

It was the beginning of an interesting journey.

A New Phase

Many broad topics were covered at the Bible Study sessions for new believers at ECU (we called it the 'Follow-Up School'). The topics included Christian choice, courtship and marriage. I attended that particular class absent-mindedly because marriage was the last thing on my mind.

I had entered the University at age fifteen and was not yet sixteen while I was in the Follow-Up school. Afterwards, I joined the Drama subgroup of the fellowship and met Olabode (the brother who would later become my husband). Also a member of the same subgroup, he became the group leader later that year.

Members of the group met to pray together often. We also went on evangelical outreaches several times and it was not too long before we had a group of praying friends.

My prayer partner was not a member of the Drama subgroup and I was surprised one day when she asked me if I had been praying about my marriage.

Taken aback, I retorted, *'I'm sixteen!'* Calmly, she replied, *'It's never too early to at least pray. It is important to have prayed before things start happening...'*, she added.

So I did pray and left it in God's hands. I told Him to lead me into the right relationship at the right time and help me to get over all my hangovers about family life.

Early in 1985, we had a Drama outreach and members of the group were to meet at a designated take-off point. Unfortunately, it was raining so badly that day that those of us who were coming from Mozambique Hall could not make it on time and the bus had to leave without us. The subgroup leader and another brother had to wait for us with another car. We got such a scolding from the leader that day that I felt like leaving the subgroup immediately.

On our way back, sitting in the bus and still unhappy about the earlier events, he came over to the window where I sat and said "I love you". I just stared at him; I couldn't say a word. I didn't know what he meant. Was he apologizing for the scolding he had given us earlier in the day or what? In any case, I decided to let it go and forgive him.

Things went back to normal for a few weeks after this until a brother showed up to propose marriage! He was a believer but I did not know him that much. I was so disturbed that I went to report him to my subgroup leader who received the news as calmly as he could and told me to pray about it.

" *I am sixteen!*" I protested.

I honestly didn't know if I wanted to pray about it. There was just something about the whole thing that made me very uneasy. I managed to pray about it and when the brother came up again to ask, I said no. I was not convinced it was right.

After this, many of my friends who had no idea what was going on kept asking me if I was praying about marriage. At this point I took the matter more seriously and would many times pray, *"Lord, I really want to know what you are saying. I know you would not leave me confused. I am still very young as you know, and marriage or even starting any relationship with that in mind is the last thing I'd like to consider at this point in time; but you know best..."*

Events took a new turn. I noticed my subgroup leader was visiting me more often and relating to me more like a friend than a subgroup leader. I had many friends - both male and female - and nothing would have been obvious then because we all visited one another to encourage and help not only in our Christian walk but also in our academics.

He was someone who loved people generally and whom everyone loved. But then, people started asking me funny questions such as if I was taking good care of him, when last did I see him, where they could find him and so on.

'This has got to stop...', I concluded. I cut down my visits and made excuses when he wanted to visit but I couldn't get round people's question. It was beginning to dawn on me that I needed to clarify with God what this all meant.

During the next few weeks, almost every time I had my quiet time, I would find that God was speaking to me about marriage. One scripture I read then said "Instead of your Father's house, shall be your people". That day I realized what God had been trying to tell me, my subgroup leader was going to be my husband. I felt a peace I could not explain and I simply left it at that.

The day after that, he came visiting and as we took a stroll down the street between Mozambique and Moremi Hall, we got talking. I told him I really wanted him to visit me less. People were talking and asking me funny questions which made me feel uncomfortable.

He wanted details and when I offered some, his response was something like, *"I had been trying to stop visiting you but I can't get myself to do it. So I prayed about it and I believe God will have me not stop."*

He paused and then asked *"supposing what people are saying or implying is what God will have for us, that is, supposing according to God's plan, we were meant for each other, would that be a problem?"*

A new relationship was birthed on June 7, 1985. It was about three months to my seventeenth birthday but I knew deep in my heart that it was right.

Many people had different opinions. My prayer partner felt the relationship was from God, and she kind of knew all along. Some people felt it would not last, considering that we were both too young (he was twenty years old).

Contrary to many people's assumptions, we both experienced God's faithfulness in many dimensions and it was a time of spiritual maturity as we learnt to do things together and faced many understandable oppositions.

Our relationship was a blessing to both of us and to many people at that time. We focused on serving God together, had many Bible study preparations together, ministered deliverance and the baptism of the Holy Ghost to others together, prayed, fasted and acted drama sketches together.

There was a two-man drama that we presented several times - just the two of us. We had the privilege of acting it at the first Mount Zion Faith Ministry Christian Drama Festival in Ibadan. There were many prophetic words about us that came through the minister who preached that day which till today are still unfolding.

He finished his Engineering degree in 1988 but I was still in Medical School. He had gone for his National Youth Service Corps (NYSC) in the then Anambra state and was coming to Ife on a visit in late 1989 when I had another deep-seated conviction in my heart that it was time to prepare for our wedding.

" Lord, I'm still in school and still very young!" I objected. When the thoughts persisted, I prayed and asked God to tell Olabode Himself. I was certainly not going to be the one to suggest a wedding at this point. It made no sense

and after all, I was the woman!

It did not surprise me when he arrived and brought up the issue. This was the beginning of another set of oppositions - particularly from our families. Their concerns were understandable. I had not finished school and my training was tedious. He was just a 'youth corper' and had no money.

My Mom had no money, neither did his Mom. Nobody could understand what the 'rush' was, so the questions started.

'Are you pregnant?'

'What do you mean God told you? How did He talk to you?'

'Why don't you just finish school?'

These were some of the many questions we were asked, but we were convinced.

It would take another book to go into the details of our beautiful wedding held at Offa, Nigeria on the 4th May, 1991. I was in my final year at the Medical School and was twenty-two years old. God showed up for us in amazing ways during the event and after.

'Our family (including our Moms and their own families)

and friends did and bought everything except for my wedding dress which Mom insisted was the duty of the groom. He had just got his salary for the first three months of work, so he graciously bought the dress so Mom could be happy. We otherwise had volunteers who would have bought it.

I had to take two weeks off my surgery posting to get married and I ended up getting the best marks in surgery during the final exams!

Married Life

After my final exams in October 1991, I moved to Lagos to join my husband who was then working at the Lagos State Water Corporation. We lived in a borrowed, one-bedroom house in Iyana Ipaja where we had our first daughter, Oluwatomi Motejumoluwa in August 1992.

Yet again, based on our convictions of God's leading, we moved to Ibadan in 1993 and had our second daughter, Titobiloluwa Oluwayinka in May 1994. We were involved together in ministry work all this while and had started having different experiences regarding family life.

I started my residency program in 1996 at the Obstetrics and Gynecology Department of the University College

Hospital, Ibadan.

My husband left for Swaziland in 1998 and we joined him in 2000 after I completed my training as an obstetrician/gynecologist - another long story that simply shows God's mercies towards us.

Oluwatimileyin Akinkunmi was born in Manzini, Swaziland in February 2002. We moved in late 2004 to South Africa to join my husband who had left Swaziland in 2001. We had our last child, Oluwatunmise Oluwafarahanmi in November 2005 in Johannesburg, South Africa. We again moved to Canada in 2008 under God's leading.

I honestly do not know how we survived the journeys and the stress on our family life, but for the grace and mercy of the almighty God! Someone recently asked if this was our final destination to which I replied, *"I don't know. Only God can decide that"*.

Our family life has had its ups and downs and what I would call severe shakings partly because of the many journeys and years of living apart. What kept us was that we were sure we were meant for each other. My husband kept saying, *"I married the right person - I have no doubts about that!"* We kept working on our differences as we raised our children the best way we knew at that time.

Our careers were tedious and demanding - mine particularly. I took more than a year-long break in 2004/2005 from clinical work to finish my Masters in Public Health (MPH) at the University of the Witwatersrand, Johannesburg, had Tunmise in 2005 November and started work in Kroonstaad, Free state in 2006 January.

By the time we relocated to Canada, I told myself I would never practice medicine again and that I was done! The many wonders and workings of God opened a door of opportunity for me to practice my profession differently in Canada, but that is yet another story. I started my own ObGyn practice in December 2009 in St. Paul, Alberta and that is what I do till date. God has been gracious!

Not long after we got to Canada, God began to open my eyes to new dimensions of what family life is supposed to be amongst Christians. He began a new work on the relationship between us and our children.

For the first time ever, we were having family discussions and realizing how far grown our first two children were. We faced this reality amidst the challenge of raising 'two sets of children' (as we refer to them) in a new culture that was very different from where we were born and where we had sojourned.

We struggled as we tried to explain the differences they were observing in our new environment and where we were coming from, using the Bible as the standard - after all my husband and I were both teachers of God's Word. God has helped us thus far.

We started a Bible Study for young adults using Skype. It involved our children, some of their cousins and friends and some of our own friends. The participants joined in from a wide geographical spread which includes St. Paul and Edmonton in Alberta; Brampton, Ontario and Kelowna, British Columbia, all in Canada. Others joined from the UK, the Caribbean Island, St. Lucia, South Africa and Nigeria. It has been a refreshing program just listening to the challenges of the young adults and trying to help them take practical Biblical decisions as they grew.

I was not too surprised when our first daughter told us she wanted to get married. Yet, it was the same set of questions: Why? What? Who? How? When? - all mostly based on our cultural inclinations.

She had friends who finished from High School the same time she did but who got married immediately after high school before they went further in training for their careers. Rather than living together as Common Law, many of the young adults in our mainly Caucasian church got married at ages ranging from nineteen to twenty-two years.

From my training and experience as a gynecologist, I knew the advantages of having children before age thirty and I have seen many older women struggle with issues of childbirth. Even in the world of science, the early twenties have proven to be the best age to start having children.

Oluwatomi got married on July 18, 2015 at age twenty-two and as at the time of writing this, Titobiloluwa is already engaged to be married at that age as well.

One of our Nigerian friends had queried, "How did you get Nigerian spouses for your daughters?" It was not an issue of nationality; it was an issue of God's choice and timing. It's not about us but God and what He is up to as regards our family life. I am just watching all the drama unfolding...

I took on the challenge of digging into issues that were affecting good family lives as God intends for believers and the first thing that came up was the fact that many of us were interpreting the scriptures from cultural mindsets.

Many of us don't bother to challenge the common conceptions about issues even when the results of such choices were not good. We simply go with the flow and criticize other believers who don't have the same viewpoints.

As I looked closer, I began to appreciate the joys of collaboration rather than competition and the fact that each nuclear and extended family was supposed to be God's perfect team to solve problems. We may be different as members of the same family but there is no superiority or inferiority interplay. We just appreciate and take advantage of God's multi-sided wisdom in embedding different gifting and abilities in each individual in the family.

Chapter 2

WHAT IS A FAMILY?

I had visited the home of one of our Nigerian family friends who also lived in Canada and heard the Mom telling one of the young adults not to consider marrying someone 'with many steps' in their household.

'What on earth does that mean?' I asked.

Her reply set me thinking.

She meant families that have too many remarried people and therefore had stepmothers, stepfathers etc. She said this presumably because the chances of stability in a new home with an individual who comes from such a background is quite low.

This got me wondering if we were talking enough about family structures and such things before our children grew up and started having relationships that may end up in marriage. I discovered that particularly as Africans, we don't define relationships well to our children and we introduce too many people to them as 'family'.

According to Google, a family can be defined as *'a group consisting of parents and children living together in a household* (a picture of the nuclear family) or *'all the descendants of a common ancestor"* (a picture of an extended family).

'Restoration' on the other hand is *"the action of returning something to a former owner, place, or condition"* or *"to repair a building, work of art etc., so that it looks as good as it did originally"*.

The original idea of the family is from God as written in the Bible. The first family began with two individuals: a male (Adam) and a female (Eve) who then had children.

> **So God created human beings in his own image. In the image of God he created them; male and female he created them. Then God blessed them and said, "Be fruitful and multiply. Fill the earth and govern it. Reign over the fish in the sea, the birds in the sky, and all the animals that scurry along the ground".**
> **Genesis 1:27-28 NLT**

The whole idea of family came from God. It is the first institution created by God. He owned the idea and He had a purpose in mind. There is no one culture or nation in the world that can claim ownership of the idea of family. Every culture borrowed the idea from God and 'modified' it to suit their purposes.

From current statistics and events in the world today, the family is a far cry from what the intention of God was as written in the Bible. I don't think any culture is left out of the poor interpretation and execution of God's family manuscript.

Despite the fact that we have the Bible which is the Owner's manual, many of us - including Bible-believing people - still interpret family issues from cultural perspectives.

God sets people in families.

> **Father to the fatherless, defender of widows–this is God, whose dwelling is holy. God places the lonely in families; he sets the prisoners free and gives them joy. But he makes the rebellious live in a sun-scorched land. Psalm 68:5-6 NLT**

Apart from Adam and Eve who were created as adults, every other human being was born as a helpless child who is highly dependent on an adult for survival.

God started the family with two adults: one male and one female. The idea is that two adults with different graces are needed to bring up their own children. God expects parents to be trainers who handle the family as a training ground to turn a child into an adult. It is God's design to

make provision for an individual until that person becomes not only independent but has the capacity to also collaborate and make provision for others.

The family serves as the smallest unit of governance under God to help a child to grow and learn basic skills for survival and independence as an adult. Learning to relate with God directly while working in a team setting is also part of God's mind for children.

A family is supposed to give each helpless little baby an identity as a starting point, a name and an automatic relationship. Every human being is born of a man and a woman, so however science played a role, ultimately every child has a biological father and a biological mother. Their children are related to them by blood. Walking away is not an option, as it does not change the DNA.

Though social and political issues come to play when it comes to raising children, the original plan as seen in the Bible is for a male adult and a female adult to come together in a unique relationship and bear and raise godly children. This is one of the reasons God hates divorce

> **Didn't the LORD make you one with your wife? In body and spirit you are his. And what does he want? Godly children from your union. So guard your heart; remain loyal to the wife of your youth. "For I hate divorce!" says the LORD, the God of Israel. "To divorce your wife is to overwhelm her with cruelty, " says the LORD of Heaven's Armies. "So guard your heart; do not be unfaithful to your wife. Malachi 2:15-16 NLT**

A Team

A team can be defined as a group of people with different skills and different tasks, who work together on a common project, service, or goal, with a meshing of functions and mutual support. (courses.washington.edu/ie337/tem.pdf)

I have not been able to come up with a better definition of a team as regards family life.

The family is a perfect example of a team. Unfortunately, when most of us think of team work, the family is not on the radar at all. More often than not, we are thinking of soccer or basketball or team activities at our workplace.

In my opinion, we have generally lost the sense of teamwork even in other systems like the health system where doctors are pitched against one another and against nurses and other healthcare workers. The purpose of healthcare which is primarily to care for the sick has been turned into a battlefield due to selfish ambitions and greed.

In the same vein, the family which is meant to be the welcoming body and trainer for new human beings just arriving into the world has become such a battlefield that the government has to step in to protect children!

The family is made up of a father, a mother and children. By design, each person is unique, important and has different sets of skills just like the human body. The analogy of the Body of Christ also describes this beautifully.

> God works in different ways, but it is the same God who does the work in all of us. A spiritual gift is given to each of us so we can help each other. - 1 Corinthians 12:6-7 NLT

> "But our bodies have many parts, and God has put each part just where he wants it. How strange a body would be if it had only one part! Yes, there are many parts, but only one body."1 Corinthians 12:18-20

> However, he has given each one of us a special gift

through the generosity of Christ. - Ephesians 4:7 NLT

The family is not made up of two fathers, ten mothers and no children. God puts each part just where He wants it and graces them for whatever role He wants them to play. He is the coach for this beautiful team and He chooses the players. They don't choose themselves; neither do they get to define their roles by who they think they are. God chooses and He graces.

Many of us believers struggle with these facts especially when there are fundamental problems in family life. God's design is that we learn how to relate with others, filling up their weaknesses with our strength and vice versa. We learn to take up roles and understand authority flow. We find out either willingly or unwillingly that family life goes beyond a solo life where it's all about the father, the mother or the children for that matter. It's about God the Creator, the Coach and the 'Gracer'.

The family can be viewed as a system and its purpose is fruitfulness or productivity. A system gives the benefit of more returns per unit work done or in other words, less work for more benefit. However, if the system is not right, there will not be much returns and in fact there could be more losses than gains. This is the reason why on the long run, some people are better off remaining single than ending up with dysfunctional families that simply adds to the current dismal statistics about the family.

Selfishness is a big issue in our world today. Of course, there is a basic instinct in every human being that seeks to put the self first, but which according to the Bible, is supposed to be changed when we receive Christ. We need to die to self as a matter of first principles in Christ. There is no way to live a fruitful and victorious life as a Christian if we keep on preserving our selfish nature. Selfishness builds a person; selflessness builds a system.

There is a common saying: "God first, others next, self-last". I believe the family is the training ground for that. The family is supposed to teach the child selflessness in the interest of the common good. That is what makes for a good church and society.

What a system consists of

Input + process = output

In Christian family terms, this means Christian male adult + Christian female adult = Christian children.

These three components form a formidable force that can

deal with any issue including financial, social, medical etc., and multiples of such families form a bedrock of a formidable church and society in the 21st century. The family has the advantage of numbers and when people have learnt to work together in groups (plural, not singular), their work is so much more effective and efficient.

> Two people are better off than one, for they can help each other succeed. If one person falls, the other can reach out and help. But someone who falls alone is in real trouble. - Ecclesiastes 4:9-10 NLT

> And five of you shall chase an hundred, and an hundred of you shall put ten thousand to flight: and your enemies shall fall before you by the sword. - Leviticus 26:8

> Children are a gift from the LORD; they are a reward from him. Children born to a young man are like arrows in a warrior's hands. How joyful is the man whose quiver is full of them! He will not be put to shame when he confronts his accusers at the city gates. - Psalms 127:3-5 NLT

Family Members

The Father

God is a father. He is the starting point and the name giver.

> **For this cause I bow my knees unto the Father of our Lord Jesus Christ, Of whom the whole family in heaven and earth is named, - Ephesians 3:14-15 KJV**

When God created the family, He wanted the adult male to behave like Him in specific relation to his nuclear family. It is a unique calling with its rights and responsibilities which God has graced men for, both anatomically and physiologically.

The dominant hormone, testosterone, is one of the graces that I believe God has given men to fulfill their roles as husband and father. It distinguishes them from the female and generally gives them some advantage like physical strength (needed to protect, do more physical work, etc.) God wants fathers to work with their wives to raise children into new fathers and mothers.

According to Wikipedia, "A father is the male parent of a (human) child". Besides the paternal bonds of a father to his children, the father has a parental, social and legal relationship with the child that carries with it certain rights and obligations, although this varies between jurisdictions.

An adoptive father is a male who has become the child's parent through the legal process of adoption.

A biological father is the male genetic contributor to the creation of the baby, through sexual intercourse or sperm donation. A biological father may have legal obligations to a child not raised by him, such as an obligation of monetary support.

A putative father is a man whose biological relationship to a child is alleged but has not been established. A stepfather is a male who is the husband of a child's mother and they may form a family unit, but who generally does not have the legal rights and responsibilities of a parent in relation to the child."

Whichever way our dictionaries have or will define 'father', it is borrowed or modified from God's definition of the word. It is an honor to be a father and God placed this honor on the adult male in the family. This, in my opinion, is the first role of a man but before this and in order to do it well, he needs to be a husband. He needs a partner, a helpmeet to bear and raise children the godly way.

As the leader in his nuclear family, he is directly

accountable to God who has placed this duty on him. The next accountability level is to his wife who is his God-given helpmeet for this specific task. Going through the pages of the Bible, the father is clearly the chief trainer of his children, not his wife. If a father is too busy to take care of his family and train his children, he is too busy!

The Mother

The mother is the female adult in the family who bears, nurtures and trains children. She is the helpmeet for the man in raising and training them. She is the manager, the soft-skill person in the family.

There should be no excuse for the adult female not to fulfill this God-given role, not her career nor her family background. The mother has been described as the button that holds the family together. The Bible says of the older women (that is, mothers):

> **The older women likewise, that they be reverent in behavior, not slanderers, not given to much wine, teachers of good things–that they admonish the young women to love their husbands, to love their children, to be discreet, chaste, homemakers, good, obedient to their own husbands, that the word of God may not be blasphemed. - Titus 2:3-5 NKJV**

And of the virtuous woman:

> She watches over the affairs of her household and does not eat the bread of idleness. - Proverbs 31:27 NIV)

The Children

For the purpose of this discussion, I will categorize the children in a nuclear family into two: the children who are underage and the adult children who are unmarried.

Underaged children have the simplest task in the family: to obey their parents. They are trainees and if they function properly, things are a lot easier for everyone in the family and the society at large. The Bible is very clear about the responsibilities of children, which is obedience.

> Children, obey your parents because you belong to the Lord, for this is the right thing to do. "Honor your father and mother." This is the first commandment with a promise: If you honor your father and mother, "things will go well for you, and you will have a long life on the earth." Ephesians 6:1-3 NLT

> Children, always obey your parents, for this pleases the Lord. - Colossians 3:20 NLT

The Adult Children

Adult children are those who have passed certain recognized landmarks - including but not exclusively - based on age and are deemed to be capable of living well as individuals.

Adult children automatically become extended family when they get married and start their own nuclear family but before then, they can still operate within their parent's nuclear family. Their roles summarily become that of support and honor, not taking over the primary responsibilities which belong to their parents.

Adult children should have obtained the capacity to work and manage money. Even if they are still living with their parents, they should pitch in and take up financial responsibilities at home. This is good training for them. No matter how small to start with, they should honor their parents with monetary gifts. This is very clear in the Bible, as the Lord Jesus states in Matthew 15.

> For instance, God says, 'Honor your father and mother,' and 'Anyone who speaks disrespectfully of father or mother must be put to death.' But you say it is all right for people to say to their parents, 'Sorry, I can't help you. For I have vowed to give to God what

> I would have given to you.' In this way, you say they don't need to honor their parents. And so you cancel the word of God for the sake of your own tradition.. - Matthew 15:4-6 NLT

> So for the sake of your tradition (the rules handed down by your forefathers), you have set aside the Word of God [depriving it of force and authority and making it of no effect]." Matthew 15:6 AMP

The first time I fully understood what this scripture is saying, I was shocked. What this literally means is that religious leaders should not stop people from giving money to their parents under the guise that such money was needed for 'God's work'.

In other words, it is very important to God that our parents are not neglected nor relegated to the background in the name of serving God. I will deal with this further in the chapter on the extended family.

Chapter 3

THE OLD AND THE NEW TESTAMENT

Going through the Bible, I have noticed very striking differences between the Old and the New Testament about many issues.

This makes it necessary to also view the family in this light. There is a clear distinction between an Old Testament person and a New Testament believer. Everything changed when Jesus Christ came on earth. The Bible says the way of thinking and relating to God as practiced in the Old Testament was faulty.

> **If the first covenant had been faultless, there would have been no need for a second covenant to replace it.. Hebrews 8:7 NLT**

It also states that some people still don't reason like New Testament believers when they read the Old Testament

> **But their minds were blinded. For until this day the same veil remains unlifted in the reading of the Old**

> Testament, because the veil is taken away in Christ. But even to this day, when Moses is read, a veil lies on their heart. Nevertheless when one turns to the Lord, the veil is taken away. II Corinthians 3:14-16 NKJV

The veil is supposed to have been taken away when one turns to Christ (Hallelujah!) Jesus came to replace the old covenant with the new. He came to give a new way of relationship with God and one another. He came to transform us and give us new ways of reasoning. I will discuss a few examples of the transformations that have taken place since Christ came.

1. In the Old Testament, a woman was worth about half the value of a man.

> Now the LORD spoke to Moses, saying, "Speak to the children of Israel, and say to them: 'When a man consecrates by a vow certain persons to the LORD, according to your valuation, if your valuation is of a male from twenty years old up to sixty years old, then your valuation shall be fifty shekels of silver, according to the shekel of the sanctuary. If it is a female, then your valuation shall be thirty shekels; and if from five years old up to twenty years old,

> then your valuation for a male shall be twenty shekels, and for a female ten shekels; and if from a month old up to five years old, then your valuation for a male shall be five shekels of silver, and for a female your valuation shall be three shekels of silver; and if from sixty years old and above, if it is a male, then your valuation shall be fifteen shekels, and for a female ten shekels.- Leviticus 27:1-7 NKJV

The New Testament approaches this differently.

> For you are all children of God through faith in Christ Jesus. And all who have been united with Christ in baptism have put on Christ, like putting on new clothes. There is no longer Jew or Gentile, slave or free, male and female. For you are all one in Christ Jesus. Galatians 3:26-28 NLT

> In the same way you married men should live considerately with [your wives], with an intelligent recognition [of the marriage relation], honoring the woman as [physically] the weaker, but [realizing that you] are joint heirs of the grace (God's unmerited favor) of life, in order that your prayers may not be hindered and cut off. [Otherwise you cannot pray effectively.] -1 Peter 3:7 AMP

I believe it's very clear that the value of both male and female are the same in the New Testament but their functions or roles are different by design.

When we reason with a mindset that both males and females have equal standing before God as clearly stated in the above scripture, then it would be easier to relate with the loving role of males and submissive role of females in a husband and wife relationship. The spiritual relationship with God remains personal and equal for both male and female.

2. In the Old Testament, divorce was simply a matter of writing a notice but this is what Jesus our Lord and Master had to say about divorce in the New Testament:

> You have heard the law that says, 'A man can divorce his wife by merely giving her a written notice of divorce.' But I say that a man who divorces his wife, unless she has been unfaithful, causes her to commit adultery. And anyone who marries a divorced woman also commits adultery. - Matthew 5:31-32 NLT

In the Old Testament, there is a long thread of dysfunctionality in families, starting from the very first one: Adam and Eve, Abraham and Sarah, then David who officially had more than one wife.

Once the effect of sin came in, it was a big struggle for human beings - male or female - to please God. The family life was not exempted. It's however unfortunate that many New Testament believers point to some of these Old Testament characters as their role models when it comes to family life. People have resorted to polygamy because Abraham had more than one wife and so did David, the man after God's heart!

We need to understand that for the New Testament believer, this kind of interpretation would be an abomination - to say the least.

The Bible is very clear that we have a better covenant, a better way of worship, a better way of relationship with God, based on better promises. We have a better solution to the problem of sin which brought the family life into such disarray right from Genesis, the book of beginnings.

We have a better capacity to obey God and live fruitful, godly lives wherever we find ourselves and in whatever situation, because we have the Holy Ghost within us. Our role model is Jesus Christ but since he never got married, we can take a cue from his earthly parents, Joseph and Mary.

The very first family that fulfilled its intended purpose according to God's plan as recorded in the New Testament was that of Joseph and Mary in bringing Jesus into the world and raising Him to fulfill His purpose. Note that they were still operating by the Old Testament standards because Jesus' blood had not been shed nor a New Testament enacted.

Joseph and Mary were operating under an inferior covenant to ours, yet they were outstanding in the fulfillment of God's heart concerning the purpose of the family. The story of Jesus' birth as recorded in the books of Matthew and Luke:

> This is how Jesus the Messiah was born. His mother, Mary, was engaged to be married to Joseph. But before the marriage took place, while she was still a virgin, she became pregnant through the power of the Holy Spirit. Joseph, her fiancé, was a good man and did not want to disgrace her publicly, so he decided to break the engagement quietly. As he considered this, an angel of the Lord appeared to him in a dream. "Joseph, son of David," the angel said, "do not be afraid to take Mary as your wife. For the child within her was conceived by the Holy Spirit. And she will have a son, and you are to name him

Jesus, for he will save his people from their sins." All of this occurred to fulfill the Lord's message through his prophet: "Look! The virgin will conceive a child! She will give birth to a son, and they will call him Immanuel, which means 'God is with us.'" When Joseph woke up, he did as the angel of the Lord commanded and took Mary as his wife. But he did not have sexual relations with her until her son was born. And Joseph named him Jesus. Matthew 1:18-25 NLT

In the sixth month of Elizabeth's pregnancy, God sent the angel Gabriel to Nazareth, a village in Galilee, to a virgin named Mary. She was engaged to be married to a man named Joseph, a descendant of King David. Gabriel appeared to her and said, "Greetings, favored woman! The Lord is with you! " Confused and disturbed, Mary tried to think what the angel could mean. "Don't be afraid, Mary," the angel told her, "for you have found favor with God! You will conceive and give birth to a son, and you will name him Jesus. He will be very great and will be called the Son of the Most High. The Lord God will give him the throne of his ancestor David. And he will reign over Israel forever; his Kingdom will

> never end!" Mary asked the angel, "But how can this happen? I am a virgin." The angel replied, "The Holy Spirit will come upon you, and the power of the Most High will overshadow you. So the baby to be born will be holy, and he will be called the Son of God. What's more, your relative Elizabeth has become pregnant in her old age! People used to say she was barren, but she has conceived a son and is now in her sixth month. For the word of God will never fail. "Mary responded, "I am the Lord's servant. May everything you have said about me come true." And then the angel left her. Luke 1:26-38 NLT

Both Joseph and Mary were individually good people. Even though they were still operating within the Old Testament system, they could relate with God personally and could hear God's instructions.

They both operated like New Testament believers and went beyond traditional concepts to obey God. Unlike most other Old Testament people, there was not one record of unbelief about them. When God's word came to them, they let God have His way.

They were not unequally yoked

Mary and Joseph had very similar core values. They both feared God and had deep respect for His words and direction.

It has been said that no matter how good an egg is, it cannot change the fact that the omelette will be bad if a bad egg is added to it (my paraphrase). The marriage of two people would not be good if their core values are different. In a situation where either the husband or the wife does not fear God or tremble at His word, their union will not be the ideal.

> **The Bible says in Amos 3:3, "Can two people walk together without agreeing on the direction?" NLT**

The Apostle Paul also referred to this in his letter to the Corinthians.

> **Don't team up with those who are unbelievers. How can righteousness be a partner with wickedness? How can light live with darkness? - 2 Corinthians 6:14 NLT**

They were both sensitive and obedient to God's leading

Mary and Joseph were visited by angels independently.

Both of them heard from God; both were willing and were instantly obedient. They functioned well as individuals in their relationship with God before they could function together as a couple.

One of the most important things to a New Testament believer is to be able to hear God. Two of the many ways this could be achieved are through dreams and visions.

Ultimately, we are all expected to be able to hear our Master's voice one way or the other. I recommend Kenneth Hagin's book, *'How to be led by the Spirit of God'*. He gave a beautiful teaching on this issue that has personally helped me understand the leading of God and the difference between the Old Testament person and the New Testament believer in this area.

Any believer should be able to seek and hear God on any specific matter and expect personal direction through any of the several ways a believer can be led by God.

> **My sheep hear my voice, and I know them, and they follow me. - John 10:27 KJV**

> **And a stranger will they not follow, but will flee from him: for they know not the voice of strangers. - John 10:5 KJV**

Sex was not the primary focus of their relationship

Even though sexual intimacy is a big part of marriage and it is a marital right, Joseph was willing to wait till Mary's God-given assignment of 'the virgin birth' was over before he claimed his 'right'. Containing our normal human passions till the appointed times is part of our training as believers.

> **God's will is for you to be holy, so stay away from all sexual sin. Then each of you will control his own body and live in holiness and honor–not in lustful passion like the pagans who do not know God and his ways.. - 1 Thessalonians 4:3-5 NLT**

There are times when believing husbands and wives also agree together to abstain from sexual intercourse for a time to focus more on prayers.

> **Do not deprive each other of sexual relations, unless you both agree to refrain from sexual intimacy for a limited time so you can give yourselves more completely to prayer. Afterward, you should come together again so that Satan won't be able to tempt you because of your lack of self-control, - 1 Corinthians 7:5 NLT**

The tendency these days is to focus on the human nature that wants immediate gratification rather than on wholesome, Biblical doctrines that encourage self-control. The need for sex has been so advertised and stretched by our world that you would think it has the same rating of necessity as the air we breathe or as water to our bodies. This is wrong.

Sexual gratification is an important part of marriage. Unfortunately, this is an issue that churches avoided talking about for so long that many Christians turned to the media for information. In the process, many got addicted to pornography! This is a far cry from the heart of God.

> **Don't copy the behavior and customs of this world, but let God transform you into a new person by changing the way you think. Then you will learn to know God's will for you, which is good and pleasing and perfect. - Romans 12:2 NLT**

Believers cannot keep thinking like the world and expect to be pleasing God.

Just as the concept of marriage is from God, the concept of sexual fulfillment is also from God and is meant to be discussed by Christians, not from the perspective of the media but from Biblical perspectives.

As an expert in my field, I know some scientific truths about hormones. They are not the reason for the sexual perversions and permissiveness we see around us. Rather, I blame it on the lack of right information with subsequent bad choices. It has to do with the mind, not the chemical substances called hormones.

Joseph and Mary had other children after our Lord Jesus who were not by virgin birth. This implies that they had a sexual life but they had to WAIT till God's purpose was fulfilled and God's timing was right.

Each performed their roles well as parents

They provided a good ground for raising Jesus, as God would want any child to be raised: to fulfill God's purpose and not some lofty human purpose. They did their part in presenting their child to God as a baby and they participated in God-focused events regularly till the child became old enough to face His calling as an individual.

After He became an adult, their roles became more subtle as parents and they became His followers. The supernatural swallowed up the natural.

> **When Jesus' parents had fulfilled all the requirements of the law of the Lord, they returned**

> home to Nazareth in Galilee. There the child grew up healthy and strong. He was filled with wisdom, and God's favor was on him. - Luke 2:39-40 NLT

Every year Jesus' parents went to Jerusalem for the Passover festival. When He was twelve years old, they attended the festival as usual.

> Then he returned to Nazareth with them and was obedient to them. And his mother stored all these things in her heart. Jesus grew in wisdom and in stature and in favor with God and all the people."- Luke 2:41-42, 51-52 NLT

Their career was not the determining factor for their lives. Their primary focus for relocating was the assignment God gave them

The first record of relocation by Joseph and Mary was when they had to take the child Jesus and flee to Egypt to protect him against King Herod's wrath.

> After the wise men were gone, an angel of the Lord appeared to Joseph in a dream. "Get up! Flee to Egypt with the child and his mother," the angel said. "Stay there until I tell you to return, because Herod is going to search for the child to kill him." That night

> Joseph left for Egypt with the child and Mary, his mother, and they stayed there until Herod's death. This fulfilled what the Lord had spoken through the prophet: "I called my Son out of Egypt. - Matthew 2:13-15 NLT

The second record of relocation was quite similar.

> When Herod died, an angel of the Lord appeared in a dream to Joseph in Egypt. "Get up!" the angel said. "Take the child and his mother back to the land of Israel, because those who were trying to kill the child are dead." So Joseph got up and returned to the land of Israel with Jesus and his mother. But when he learned that the new ruler of Judea was Herod's son Archelaus, he was afraid to go there. Then, after being warned in a dream, he left for the region of Galilee. So the family went and lived in a town called Nazareth. This fulfilled what the prophets had said: "He will be called a Nazarene. - Matthew 2:14, 19-23 NLT

The major movements of this family were to fulfill scriptures and protect the destiny of the child Jesus. They performed all the Old Testament requirements in presenting Jesus for dedication at the temple, taking him to

Jerusalem for the Passover, etc. Still, they strike me as cutting-edge, right-on-time 'listeners to God's voice' kind of people who heard God's voice and followed his direction per time.

The Bible says *"as many as are led by the Spirit of God, they are the sons of God"*. These were sons of God operating under an inferior covenant. The New Testament believers have a better covenant, yet many of us are led by media predictions, career demands, economic crises, personal pursuits for money and fame and many other reasons rather than godly instructions.

In my opinion, we get not only ourselves but also our entire families into many avoidable problems.

> **Those who bring trouble on their families inherit the wind. The fool will be a servant to the wise. - Proverbs 11:29 NLT**

These days, many families relocate or are torn apart only for career purposes. This happens even in Christian families.

I believe that as New Testament believers, hearing God clearly and putting the family first should be the main reason for such big steps and not career.

Many institutions have also broken up and destroyed families because of the level of expectations and demands placed on individuals within them. This has not added to building good societies. Rather, it is mostly responsible for the chaos our world has found itself in presently.

Career building is good if it is for the purpose of enhancing family life and not destroying it.

I have personal testimonies of the times when I had to stop work, refocus and get refreshed before recommencing what I do. I have never regretted creating such times deliberately. My emphasis is on the fact that we need to focus on being led by the Spirit of God as a matter of priority in family matters

> **All Scripture is inspired by God and is useful to teach us what is true and to make us realize what is wrong in our lives. It corrects us when we are wrong and teaches us to do what is right.. - 2 Timothy 3:16 NLT**

All scripture - both the Old and the New Testament - is inspired by God but we need to interpret and apply them differently as led by the Spirit of God. We need to rightly explain the Word of God in a balanced way and in right context. We cannot pattern our family lives after people in the Old Testament who obviously failed God in many respects.

> Work hard so you can present yourself to God and receive his approval. Be a good worker, one who does not need to be ashamed and who correctly explains the word of truth." - 2 Timothy 2:15 NLT

Chapter 4

THE EXTENDED FAMILY

There is a big issue in many African cultures about the extended family and their role.

I do not see much of this where I currently live because they seem to have more clearly defined boundaries. They have their own issues, but such are not as bad as what we struggle with in Africa.

I was curious and eager to find solutions from the Bible which can be applied to any cultural setting with the certainty of getting results. These are some of the answers I got:

The nuclear family according to the definition quoted in the first chapter of this book is "a group consisting of parents and children living together in a household".

In Christian family terms, this will mean a father, mother and children. I am of the opinion that this includes underage children who are still dependent on adults for provision of their daily needs such as food, clothing, shelter, training etc. This excludes children who are grown up and can live their lives independently.

In other words, our adult children become extended family once they grow up. This becomes more established when they marry and start their own nuclear families.

This was a hard truth to swallow (particularly for my husband) when our first daughter got married. We all had to come to terms with the fact that this understanding would make for proper boundaries and healthy relationships hereafter.

The Adult Child

Who is an adult child?

This is another question with different answers, depending on cultural perspectives. Age has mostly been the yardstick for defining adulthood in many cultures. In Canada, an 18-year-old person is an adult and can vote and be voted for. He or she can make decisions without parental consent.

Personally, I feel that this age is rather young to take important life decisions alone. I have seen many people struggle and make bad choices as they left their parents at this age immediately after high school.

I also discovered that many of our African friends felt this was not acceptable in their cultures but they had no defined age for adulthood. A 'child' could live and feed off the parents till age thirty without much problems! I don't think this is right either and I believe it is actually the cause of many 'extended family' issues that can be avoided.

Looking through the Bible I tried to find a common ground. What age would be the most appropriate?

I did not find any clue in the New Testament and this is probably because the written laws of dos and don'ts has been replaced by a superior one where one has the Spirit of God and there is more flexibility. The Bible however states that the Old Testament had a form of worship that was the shadow of things to come.

> **The old system under the law of Moses was only a shadow, a dim preview of the good things to come, not the good things themselves. The sacrifices under that system were repeated again and again, year after year, but they were never able to provide perfect cleansing for those who came to worship. - Hebrews 10:1 NLT**

For the Jews who were exclusively the people of God in the Old Testament, age twenty was the age of adulthood when certain responsibilities were demanded of them - including paying temple taxes and defending their nation as soldiers.

> **From the whole community of Israel, record the names of all the warriors by their clans and families. List all the men twenty years old or older who are able to go to war. You and Aaron must register the troops. - Numbers 1:2-3**

> **In accordance with David's final instructions, all the Levites twenty years old or older were registered for service. - 1 Chronicles 23:27 NLT**

I found age twenty reasonable to work with.

First of all, a twenty-year-old has passed the teenage years which has the proven characteristics of turbulence, both emotionally and in decision making. The teenage brain is yet to be fully developed in the area of executive reasoning and so decisions made at this point of life are often irrational and not well thought-through. At age eighteen, the young lady or man has just finished high school (in most cases) and will start gathering experience on working and making things work.

With our two adult children, we made sure they started filing taxes at age eighteen even though they were in the university. By age twenty, this had become routine for both of them. In particular, our daughter who studied accounting was handling the family business and keeping the books at the same time. Both of them entered college before age eighteen and budgeting became part of their routines as soon as they left home for college

The Transition Process

Transitioning from childhood into adulthood is a tedious process and every family needs the grace and mercy of God as we watch our children grow. We must work with them to make right choices about such things as career paths but of first importance, marriage.

I came from a background where career obviously was promoted over and above marriage. As I grew up and observed the outcomes of decisions in many families, I realized a flaw in this perspective. It is like insisting that life happens in a certain premeditated order: a child grows up, goes to and finishes school, starts working and gets married to the right person at the right time and they settle down in the best place (in the opinion of their parents who by the way, also have different opinions).

We all know life doesn't happen that way all the time - no

matter how hard parents try.

In my family, we learnt to allow the children grow in God's hands and with the perspective that He (God), would take care of them as they committed their lives to Him, after all, God has no grandchildren! In the same way that I believe He will take care of me since I am His child, He will also take care of them.

Thus, we let them grow up, take decisions and take responsibility for their decisions as they learn to relate with God on a one on one basis. Without insisting on a particular order, we gave advice and prayed for them and God has always been there for us.

So technically, we have two extended family members. Though born by us, they do not depend on us for their daily lives and needs like food and clothing. Neither do they depend on us for their everyday decisions. Now we relate like brethren in Christ. They don't have to always follow our instructions like the other two that are underage. They don't even have to take our advice all the time and we don't feel bad about that.

The most important lesson I have learnt so far is that God has plans for them that are much better than what I can imagine for them and He will get them there.

We are blessed that they both chose to follow Jesus as individuals, not as part of the family crowd.

Thus, the term 'extended family' is not a far-fetched concept like great grandparents or distant uncles. Any member of the family who has grown beyond the nuclear family is part of the extended family and the rules that govern successful relationships differ in each circumstance.

Except for Adam and Eve, every nuclear family came from another nuclear family. Every extended family started out as a nuclear family comprising a father, mother and children. Each nuclear family is unique and accountable to God directly. Children are to obey their own parents in their nuclear families as a matter of first importance, and not their extended family. Wives are to be submissive to their own husbands and not to every male who seeks to dominate them.

Every Christian couple and subsequently nuclear family, has an autonomy that is meant to be respected by members of the extended family.

One of the most important factors in a successful family life is that the man has 'left' his father and mother. He now has the capacity to cleave to his own wife and not to his mother who happens to be his father's wife and not his. He is to lead his own nuclear family.

The extended family can of course advise, help, support but they are not meant to instruct or dominate. The Bible says 'train a child in the way he should go' and not 'train an adult' particularly one who has his own nuclear family already.

Chapter 5

CHILDREN

> Children are a gift from the LORD; they are a reward from him. Children born to a young man are like arrows in a warrior's hands. How joyful is the man whose quiver is full of them! He will not be put to shame when he confronts his accusers at the city gates. - Psalm 127:3-5 NLT

Children are a gift and not a burden!

One of the problems that I have seen in our world today is that the church has in general adopted the mind-set of the world as a yardstick for either having or raising children.

The mind-set of the civilized world is that children are a burden to raise and expensive to maintain. In fact, many people treat their own children as distractions to focusing on their careers. I was pleasantly surprised to find out that in rural Alberta where I currently live, many women bear and raise their children to school age before they resume their career paths.

I grew up in a culture where there is a lot of emphasis on career to the detriment of the family - particularly where raising young children are concerned.

The longest I stayed with any of my children before I went back to work was two months whereas where we currently live, you could have up to one-year maternity leave. In fact, many workplaces give paternity leave as well. I wish I came here earlier!

When we started our family, three children seemed to be the norm amongst our own Christian peers, so having four children was something like going a bit above board. Anything more than four children was considered 'too much' and the educated society around us did not make it any easier.

I am an obstetrician/gynaecologist by profession and I have four children. The reaction I get from a lot of people is, "How on earth are you coping?" My answer is simple: God's grace has always been sufficient for me and where there is a will, there is way.

Despite a very tedious work routine when I was having my babies, I exclusively breastfed the four of them for at least four months each before adding some adult food. I breastfed each for at least one year and never gave any one of them infant formula feeds. They all grew up healthy.

Choosing a tedious career like mine almost meant either not getting married or not having children, not to talk of four!

The number of children each couple should have should not be determined by the way the world system thinks. Just as God is interested in whom each adult will marry, He is interested in how many children each will have, when they start having them, how they raise them, where to live, what career would work best for the parents and on and on.

I believe having children should be well planned by every couple under God's guidance. We should avoid the two extremes of either thinking family planning is a sin, or that children are a burden and the less, the better.

If a couple decides to have ten children and raise them well, they should not be seen as less spiritual than a couple who decides to have one child. 'Be fruitful and multiply' is still God's original instruction despite our man-made problems.

I honestly do not see how deliberately just having a child to maintain a career, political correctness or a good figure fulfils the multiplication mandate given by God.

Many Christians have become so selfish in their reasoning that you wonder where their ideology came from. Some determine outright never to have children for no special reason at all. The world's system is not helping matters concerning family life; must we join them?

I suggest a particular message by Voddi Baucham on the centrality of the home (on YouTube), it offers some mind blowing statistics about birth rates as it affects our Christian families and specific societal issues. It also confirmed some of the convictions I've had for a long time about raising children and offers food for thought in preventing further damage to our attitudes towards family life.

My ideology about children was first challenged in 2000 by a young African doctor who just got married at that time. I had asked him about how many children they plan to have. He replied, 'Six at least' and my reaction was, "You must be joking!" But he was not joking at all.

He explained to me that he had observed that families with the capacity to train children well and who have the resources to give children the best education end up having just one or two while those who are less privileged have about ten. He went on to say those well trained two kids of yours will have to work extra hard and pay enough taxes for the ten that are untrained to maintain a balance in their society when they become adults.

He further added that he knew that as a doctor from his kind of background, he would probably have to pay for the education of ten children anyway because of the needs and demands from relatives, so why not let at least six of them be his own children?

This was the first time I was hearing this kind of opinion from an educated person, I used to think it was illiterates who reasoned this way!

In the scripture quoted above, when children are born to a young man who still has the strength and zest to play with them and train them, they are given the capacity to become the family's asset for ever. They will be there to protect the interests of the family, honor their parents and stand as a formidable force in the building of the society.

Statistics have shown that in countries where having children was taken out of the control of individual families and couples were not having 'enough' babies, their economies started crumbling because they did not have enough workforce to keep their systems going. Many of such countries are highly dependent on immigrants -

whether they like that fact or not.

Children are a good and important part of the family with specific, God-given roles, whether they are still children or adults.

The Divorce Challenge

God wants godly children from couples. One of the reasons He hates divorce is because the children are badly affected.

> **Didn't the LORD make you one with your wife? In body and spirit you are his. And what does he want? Godly children from your union. So guard your heart; remain loyal to the wife of your youth. "For I hate divorce!" says the LORD, the God of Israel. "To divorce your wife is to overwhelm her with cruelty," says the LORD of Heaven's Armies. "So guard your heart; do not be unfaithful to your wife. - Malachi 2:15-16 NLT**

Divorce is a painful process which can be avoided. It is not the easy way out like it has been painted by the media. Nobody who has seen the devastating effects of divorce would wish their children would go through the same ordeal.

While it is true that many Christians - including preachers - have gone through divorce, the truth of God's word is that He hates divorce. I do not believe any Christian would particularly love divorce. I see it as an unfortunate fix to problems that are better prevented.

While in some circumstances I admit that divorce is inevitable, we should bring up our children to hate it just as God does and to avoid the same pitfalls that lead to divorce amongst Christians. The world may have many authentic reasons for the rising divorce rates but this should never be a Christian phenomenon.

Most importantly, the church should focus more on preventing further damage rather than condemning the people who are unfortunate enough to have gone through it. My parents got divorced when I was 7 years old so I am no stranger to what the effects could be on children, but I am also overwhelmingly convinced of God's healing power through Jesus Christ - no matter how terrible the situation is.

Parenthood

To deal with children with a Biblical mindset is a challenge in our present day where the governments of different countries and cultures have created environments for abuse of parenthood. Let's look at some scriptures and what I mean by abuse of parenthood.

> **Train up a child in the way he should go, And when he is old he will not depart from it. - Proverbs 22:6 NKJV**

> **Teach children how they should live, and they will remember it all their life. - Proverbs 22:6 GNT**

Children are meant to be trained by their families, not the government. The family is the smallest unit of governance under God and many times when God made definite changes in human history, He used the parents to raise their children properly under His directions.

The core values of life such as honesty, hard work, understanding authority and participating effectively in teams are best taught to children by their parents. The unfortunate thing however, is that many families do not have the time or the capacity to play their roles well. We often pay teachers to do what only parents can do, and we end up confusing the children about what is right and wrong.

Recently, a bill was to be passed where I live currently that would allow children to choose their genders from elementary school! The Bible is clear on the general behaviour of children.

> **Children just naturally do silly, careless things, but a good spanking will teach them how to behave... - Proverbs 22:15 GNTD**

> **A youngster's heart is filled with foolishness, but physical discipline will drive it far away. - Proverbs 22:15 NLT**

> **Woe to thee, O land, when thy king is a child, and thy princes eat in the morning! - Ecclesiastes 10:16 KJV**

Children naturally think of and do silly things. This is normal and that is why they need adults to be there with them and train them the way they should go.

Children are not meant to choose their genders, just as they are not allowed to choose whether or not to smoke cigarettes or take alcohol before they are adults! They are meant to be trained and raised up by their parents. We are simply calling for more societal problems if we allow the children 'to rule, pick and choose' with their naturally immature mind sets.

Having said these, I do realize that there are exceptional cases where the words of a child can bring positive influences and change, but that is the exception rather than the rule.

Let me stress this again: the church should not replace Biblical teachings with the New Age concepts that major on the minors and minor on the majors. Woe to the land where the word of the children is the rule.

I often tell my children to wait till they are adults when they want to dictate how much we spend on what at home and things like what I cook for the family. It's only fair: I waited for my turn to make such decisions.

I believe one of the issues to discuss further is the extreme stances that different cultures have taken when it comes to child discipline. Discipline and training are not the same thing. Discipline is only a part of training while training would include other things like giving instructions, teaching and showing them examples they can follow.

The Bible's stance is very clear about discipline:

> **Those who spare the rod of discipline hate their children. Those who love their children care enough to discipline them. - Proverbs 13:24 NLT**

> If you don't punish your children, you don't love them. If you do love them, you will correct them.. - Proverbs 13:24 GNTD

> Don't hesitate to discipline children. A good spanking won't kill them. As a matter of fact, it may save their lives. - Proverbs 23:13, 14 GNTD

> Don't fail to discipline your children. They won't die if you spank them. Physical discipline may well save them from death. - Proverbs 23:13, 14 NLT

> Correction and discipline are good for children. If they have their own way, they will make their mothers ashamed of them. - Proverbs 29:15 GNTD

The Bible is also very explicit about training children:

> Parents, do not treat your children in such a way as to make them angry. Instead, raise them with Christian discipline and instruction. - Ephesians 6:4 GNTD

> Fathers, do not provoke your children to anger by the way you treat them. Rather, bring them up with the discipline and instruction that comes from the Lord. - Ephesians 6:4 NLT

> And have you forgotten the encouraging words God

> spoke to you as his children? He said, "My child, don't make light of the LORD's discipline, and don't give up when he corrects you. For the LORD disciplines those he loves, and he punishes each one he accepts as his child." As you endure this divine discipline, remember that God is treating you as his own children. Who ever heard of a child who is never disciplined by its father? If God doesn't discipline you as he does all of his children, it means that you are illegitimate and are not really his children at all. - **Hebrews 12:5-8 NLT**

Discipline and abuse are not the same thing. I believe many governments started promulgating laws to protect children as a reaction to the bad ways some families were treating their children. However, an extreme of this child protection principle is to say children should not be disciplined at all or that they should be allowed to choose their genders!

Taking a closer look at some of these laws that prohibit child discipline, I discovered that there are extreme interpretations as well. For instance, in one of the provinces of Canada, the law says not to beat a child on the head, face, genitals or leave marks on the body of the child - which honestly makes sense. It did not say not to spank the child - which is the extreme interpretation some people have given this law.

Sometimes the problem is that we believe so much in correcting by the rod that we do it to adults! A father trying to beat an eighteen year old or even a twelve year old who is already taller than himself is looking for more trouble than solutions. Children are best corrected with spanking when they are children, not adults. Other methods of discipline would work better for older children who were spanked when they were younger, than for untrained, older children.

The other extreme is to let the children grow without any form of discipline or corrective measures at all. Such children often turn out to hate the parents and become uncultured members of the society - which is not what any government wants anyway.

Whatever the situation, we should avoid being extremists in raising or disciplining our children.

Adult Children

Adult children are those who have passed certain recognized landmarks including but not exclusively based on age and are deemed to be capable of living well as individuals. They will forever be our children but they cannot be treated the same way as we would treat underage children.

At this point we can give advice, be their coach, mentor or friend - depending on what kind of relationship has been built over their years of growing up. Respect should be mutual and boundaries should be respected particularly for the married ones. They do not depend on us anymore for sustenance and their role is to honor their parents in whatever capacity they can, not to take over the parents' responsibilities as indicated by God. They do not have to obey every instruction we give and we are not the controller of their lives; God is. The sooner this is realized, the better for all parties.

There are various ways that honor can be bestowed on parents and grandparents by their adult children but I will share a few thoughts from the Bible

Adult children are meant to care for their parents or grandparents who have problems of lack of basic daily needs. In God's family of believers, there should be no lack and as such, the church is entrusted with gathering and distributing resources for the poor particularly amongst its members. This is the reason why there should be a list of widows who are in need.

However, anyone who is truly in need but have children or grandchildren who are believers should not be placed on that list. Such a person should be taken care of by their adult children or relative and the church should be spared the burden of taking care of such a person. This is a way to honor our parents, grandparents or extended family members.

> Take care of any widow who has no one else to care for her. But if she has children or grandchildren, their first responsibility is to show godliness at home and repay their parents by taking care of them. This is something that pleases God. 1Tim. 5:3-4 NLT

Looking closely, that scripture does not include children of relatives (who are meant to be taken care of by their own parents), nor parents who are working or can work to provide for their daily needs. It also does not put the burden of providing luxuries as a compulsory part of the package. The Bible encourages giving what we have, not what we don't.

> Whatever you give is acceptable if you give it eagerly. And give according to what you have, not what you don't have. - 2 Corinthians 8:12 NLT

> Therefore, whenever we have the opportunity, we

> should do good to everyone to those in the family of faith. - Galatians 6:10 NLT

The Bible also recognizes and encourages adult children to give back to their parents, and not necessarily because the parents are in need.

> For God commanded, Honor your father and your mother, and, He who curses or reviles or speaks evil of or abuses or treats improperly his father or mother, let him surely come to his end by death. [Exod. 20:12; 21:17; Lev. 20:9; Deut. 5:16.]

> But you say, If anyone tells his father or mother, What you would have gained from me [that is, the money and whatever I have that might be used for helping you] is already dedicated as a gift to God, then he is exempt and no longer under obligation to honor and help his father or his mother. So for the sake of your tradition (the rules handed down by your forefathers), you have set aside the Word of God [depriving it of force and authority and making it of no effect]. - Matthew 15:4-6 AMP

We are to honor our parents with monetary gifts and other things like being present to celebrate events that are important to the family, sharing our time with them when they need it most. This is a good cycle that should continue through many generations. It will relieve the governments who are already struggling with the huge task of taking care of so many elderly people - particularly in aging populations which by the way are man-made.

God still cares and expects His people to help solve the problems of the world and not add to them.

Underage Children

The role of the underage children is to obey their parents, carry out instructions and help to keep the household functioning properly. Put simply, honoring their parents mean obeying them. A child's duty is to be trained to be independent and able to support not only his/her nuclear family but to help his/her extended family and support other worthy causes. This is called 'capacity building' and is an essential part of building efficient systems.

> **Children, obey your parents because you belong to the Lord, for this is the right thing to do. "Honor your father and mother." This is the first commandment with a promise: If you honor your father and mother, "things will go well for you, and you will have a long life on the earth."** - Ephesians 6:1-3 NLT

> **Children, always obey your parents, for this pleases the Lord. - Colossians 3:20 NLT**

Obedience is a command from God, not an option. The world system already promotes an atmosphere of rebellion.

The media often makes it seem as if defiance to authorities (particularly to parents) works better than otherwise. What they fail to realize is that children who are brought up to disobey their parents will never learn obedience to any authority (including governments) and will ultimately be a problem to the entire society.

The role of children is simple: obey and respect your parents, pitch up and do your duties at home, be trained in the art of living a fulfilled life as an adult.

The rights of children are also clear. They should be loved, provided for and trained. God gives grace for every particular role played by different family members, and children are no exception.

Chapter 6

BLUEPRINTS FOR AN ADULT CHRISTIAN LIFE

I grew up as a young adult with conflicting ideas about marriage and family. I did not have many examples around me of a perfect family. But for the grace and mercy of God, we would all have been consumed.

I am writing this chapter particularly for the young adult Christian who is seeking to know what foundation to build on to achieve their dreams in life.

Make sure you marry right. Your career is not as important as your marriage. With a career, you may have multiple choices and different opportunities. In marriage, you basically have one. Male or female, your marriage could make or mar you and it deserves attention early enough in life.

You may be asking, 'How early?' As early as you realize how important it is to be married right. The age of maturity varies widely but it is never too early to start praying that God will help you pick the right person at the right time and in the right place. Don't leave considerations about marriage till when you are too old or too desperate.

There are many books that talk about how to choose the right person and the aim of this book is not to teach on that primarily. However, there are a few tips I would like to drop.

1. Don't marry an unbelieving person. It is not worth the effort. You don't want the devil as your father-in-law.

2. Find out the difference between Biblical expectations and cultural expectations and aim to please God. It is more difficult to please people than to please God.

3. Give family life the focus it deserves. Nothing just happens by chance. It takes effort and commitment to start and maintain a family.

The Biblical way to finding God

Finding God is the most important thing in life and it is a very personal experience. It cannot be obtained by inheritance or by training at school.

When you make God first in everything and choose to please Him in your decision making, you are guaranteed a fulfilled life of purpose and impact. Jesus has to be your personal savior and Lord and not just the God of your parents or forefathers. Your relationship with him and how well you hear Him should by all means precede important decisions like whom you commit your life to in marriage.

> Jesus answered him, I assure you, most solemnly I tell you, that unless a person is born again (anew, from above), he cannot ever see (know, be acquainted with, and experience) the kingdom of God. - John 3:3 AMP

> Remember the Lord in everything you do, and he will show you the right way. Never let yourself think that you are wiser than you are; simply obey the Lord and refuse to do wrong. - Proverbs 3:6-7 GNT

> Don't copy the behavior and customs of this world, but let God transform you into a new person by changing the way you think. Then you will learn to know God's will for you, which is good and pleasing and perfect. - Romans 12:2 NLT

The Biblical way to finding a wife

Ask God and let Him help you choose. You do not get to choose your parents, siblings or children. Your spouse is the only family member you get to choose; so take your time and choose well. Let your mentors and family members participate to the extent that is necessary, but realize that ultimately, the choice is yours. You are the one who is going to live with this person and both of you will have to work things out together.

> **A man can inherit a house and money from his parents, but only the Lord can give him a sensible wife. - Proverbs 19:14 GNT**

> Find a wife and you find a good thing; it shows that the Lord is good to you. - Proverbs 18:22 GNT

The Biblical way to finding a career

A career is meant to be what you do for a living. The best career that will suit you is one that draws on your innate abilities and makes you useful to the people around you. It is what you do to contribute to the progress of humanity and at the same time, it's what will give you back enough money to live a good life.

Career choice should not be based on how much money you can make from a particular profession. Any believer can be rich doing any kind of work, as long as that is the area of his or her calling. The prosperity promised by God will be obvious to all. So our ambition is not to pick a profession that will make us rich or famous but according to the scriptures, our ambition should be as follows:

> ...and to make it your ambition to lead a quiet life: You should mind your own business and work with your hands, just as we told you, so that your daily life may win the respect of outsiders and so that you will not be dependent on anybody. – 1Thessalonians 4:11-12 NIV

Or in other words...

> Make it your aim to live a quiet life, to mind your own business, and to earn your own living, just as we told you before. In this way you will win the respect of those who are not believers, and you will not have to depend on anyone for what you need. – 1 Thessalonians 4:11-12 GNT

> Whatever you do, do well. For when you go to the grave, there will be no work or planning or knowledge or wisdom. – Ecclesiastes 9:10 NLT

> I have observed something else under the sun. The fastest runner doesn't always win the race, and the strongest warrior doesn't always win the battle. The wise sometimes go hungry, and the skillful are not

> necessarily wealthy. And those who are educated don't always lead successful lives. It is all decided by chance, by being in the right place at the right time.
> **Ecclesiastes 9:11 NLT**

According to the observation of King Solomon in the book of Ecclesiastes, everything in life is decided by being at the right place at the right time.

The advantage that believers have is that we have the God-factor which makes us to be at the right place at the right time. We do not leave things to chance. When we take our lives into our hands and make choices from only what we can see and hear and feel, we rob ourselves of this advantage and in the end, we get the results the general populace get.

Aim to please God and serve humanity the best way you can, and you will be rich as a believer.

Making mistakes is part of the process of learning but even when that happens, God makes all things work together for our good.

The Biblical way to serve God

This sounds like a paradox!

'Serving God' surely must be Biblical, no matter how we look at it. Would that statement be correct? I have seen many people claiming to serve God but without the proofs that accompany servants of God.

There are two broad categories of service in the ministry: full time (career) or part time (tent making). I will use the examples of Apostles Paul and Peter in the Bible.

Peter was specifically called by Jesus to be an apostle to the Jews, whilst Paul was called as an apostle to the Gentiles. Jesus emphatically told Peter to drop his fishing career whilst Paul carried out his apostolic service while also working with his own hands and receiving occasional financial support for his ministry work. Peter was married and sometimes took his wife with him on ministry travels while Paul was never married.

The question is, who was better, Peter or Paul? The correct answer is this: both were the best because they were designed and called for the kind of life they lived.

There are no grounds for comparison here and no minister is better than the other in terms of how we serve God. We are simply different and that is God's design. As we have already established, God calls, God graces.

When we try to compare ourselves and decide for ourselves if and when to go into full time ministry as a career, we run into problems. Every believer - married or single - should be serving God, whatever their calling is. A family man or woman, whether in full time ministry or tent making ministry, has financial and other obligations to his family that he/she cannot be excused from.

If we get these principles clear from the onset, we can truly expect to live the abundant life that the Lord promised, otherwise we will find that the yoke we are bearing and making our families to bear is difficult and not fulfilling.

Some people go into full time ministry because they think it is a better way to serve God. There is no better way, only the best way - which is the way of God's specific calling for each believer.

> **What, after all, is Apollos? And what is Paul? Only servants, through whom you came to believe – as the Lord has assigned to each his task. I planted the seed, Apollos watered it, but God has been making it grow. So then, no more boasting about human leaders! All things are yours, whether Paul or Apollos or Cephas or the world or life or death or the present or the futureare yours, and you are of Christ, and**

Christ is of God. 1 Corinthians 3:5-6, 21-23 NIV

A believer's ministry and mode of service to God may also change over time. For example, Paul the apostle started out as one of the teachers and prophets in Antioch before he and Barnabas were called out from among others to be apostles on a specific mission.

> **Among the prophets and teachers of the church at Antioch of Syria were Barnabas, Simeon (called "the black man"), Lucius (from Cyrene), Manaen (the childhood companion of King Herod Antipas), and Saul. One day as these men were worshiping the Lord and fasting, the Holy Spirit said, "Dedicate Barnabas and Saul for the special work to which I have called them." So after more fasting and prayer, the men laid their hands on them and sent them on their way. - Acts of the Apostles 13:1-3 NLT**

Summarily, serving God may take different forms at different times in a believer's life. The bottom line is to know that each of us has been called to a life of service to God which also takes into account the fact that service to God includes taking care of our families as a matter of priority.

The late Dr. Myles Munroe would say, "The Bible says love

your wife as Christ loved his own wife (the church). Don't love Jesus' wife more than yours, he didn't ask you to!"

Resource Management

Live well - be happy!

Happiness is a byproduct of fruitful service. Joy is a God-given product that comes from a spirit-controlled life. Your aim should not be to go out looking for who will make you happy but whom you will make happy and in return happiness comes back to you. It's a strange phenomenon that depression is becoming common amongst believers. As the song goes, "We are happy people, praise the Lord!"

Eat well, work hard, exercise well and rest well. Be healthy and aim to live a balanced life from the onset. It is better to prevent the problem of a cluttered life than to want to get rid of clutter later in life.

In order to lead a productive life as a Christian, aim to live a balanced life. Balance your spiritual life, family life and career in that order. Take care of your spirit, soul and body in that order, realizing that balance is an art that is continuously learnt and practiced throughout life. What it takes for a young adult to be balanced is different from what it takes for someone much older. Let God help you and don't compare yourself with others. Each Christian is unique and we all have unique callings.

> Of course we would not dare classify ourselves or compare ourselves with those who rate themselves so highly. How stupid they are! They make up their own standards to measure themselves by, and they judge themselves by their own standards! - 2 Corinthians 10:12 GNT

On a general note, God's intention about our welfare is clear in the Bible — to be prosperous and happy

> Beloved, I pray that you may prosper in every way and [that your body] may keep well, even as [I know] your soul keeps well and prospers. - 3 John 1:2 AMP

> Live happily with the woman you love through all the meaningless days of life that God has given you under the sun. The wife God gives you is your reward for all your earthly toil. - Ecclesiastes 9:9 NLT

> So I concluded there is nothing better than to be happy and enjoy ourselves as long as we can. And people should eat and drink and enjoy the fruits of their labor, for these are gifts from God. Ecclesiastes 3:12-13 NLT

Money: Learning how to make it and what to do with it

Money making and money management are two different skills that many people do not have. If they do have it, they have just one of the two.

The Bible makes it very clear that we must seek God first and not money. We must serve God and not money. I highly recommend Kenneth Hagin's book, The Midas Touch. It is the most balanced teaching about prosperity I have ever read or heard.

Money is good and I have experienced both poverty and riches and concluded that you can live a much more productive life when you can make money and manage it well. People whose sole aim in life is to be rich often miss the mark, but believers who work according to divine principles will have riches following them, running after them and overtaking them. The latter is better than the former. I have so many personal testimonies along these lines that it may take us off point to start discussing them here.

In one of his letters to Timothy, Paul wrote about certain believers.

> These people always cause trouble. Their minds are

corrupt, and they have turned their backs on the truth. To them, a show of godliness is just a way to become wealthy. Yet true godliness with contentment is itself great wealth. After all, we brought nothing with us when we came into the world, and we can't take anything with us when we leave it. So if we have enough food and clothing, let us be content. But people who long to be rich fall into temptation and are trapped by many foolish and harmful desires that plunge them into ruin and destruction. For the love of money is the root of all kinds of evil. And some people, craving money, have wandered from the true faith and pierced themselves with many sorrows. - 1 Timothy 6:5-10 NLT

The Bible also says

No one can serve two masters. For you will hate one and love the other; you will be devoted to one and despise the other. You cannot serve both God and money. - Matthew 6:24 NLT

Don't wear yourself out trying to get rich. Be wise enough to know when to quit.. - Proverbs 23:4 NLT

The blessing of the Lord —it makes [truly] rich, and He adds no sorrow with it [neither does toiling increase it]. - Proverbs 10:22 AMP

Time

Time is the one resource that God gave to everybody in equal amount. Everybody has got 24 hours in a day: no more, no less. No one is richer than the other in this respect. People who have learnt to manage their time well achieve so much more in life.

The Bible says there is a time for everything. God wants us to make the best use of this resource and learning how to do this early in life will not only make your life peaceful but will affect those around you positively.

Prioritizing is a must for every believer in the 21st century and we need to understand that what we value most naturally tends to take most of our time. Start with an audit of how much time you spend on what per day and it will give you an idea of what you value most.

Family life is very important to God and if you are too busy to attend to your family obligations and responsibilities, then you are too busy!

> **For everything there is a season, a time for every activity under heaven.. Ecclesiastes 3:1 NLT**

> Make the most of every opportunity in these evil days. Don't act thoughtlessly, but understand what the Lord wants you to do. - Ephesians 5:16-17 NLT

Physical Energy

> Don't let the excitement of youth cause you to forget your Creator. Honor him in your youth before you grow old and say, "Life is not pleasant anymore. - Ecclesiastes 12:1 NLT

> "The glory of the young is their strength; the gray hair of experience is the splendor of the old." Proverbs 20:29 NLT

The glory of the youth is indeed their strength. I cannot forget the days of Christian fellowship when we were in the University. We were stretched and trained in the things of God beyond what we would have imagined we could handle. We had long fasts and prayed long prayers. Male or female, we carried heavy loads and walked long distances to participate in what God was doing in that dispensation.

We did all these in the sun and in the rain, whether it was convenient or not, and we came out excelling not only in spiritual things but also in our academics.

Many of us are successful full time ministers, professionals and businessmen today with a lot of positive outcomes to our decision to follow Jesus wholeheartedly. I encourage every young adult to serve God with the strength you have whilst you still have it. It pays off.

God's Institutions for Training

There are three institutions created by God for the training and governance of human beings. The first is the family, the next is the church and the last is the government.

The Family: Ideally, your nuclear family is your default team. It's the place where you get your core values from. When you become an adult and start your own nuclear family, they become extended family. You should no longer depend on them for existence but God still expects an ongoing relationship with them. The extended family beautifully fits in as those we can go to for advice, loans, physical help, ceremonies, etc., and they are the first group to give back to.

The Church: Ideally, you should go to a church where you can form social links with people who believe the Bible is the Word of God, learn more about God and His people and collaborate with others to advance the Kingdom of

God. The role of the pastor of a local assembly is not to replace that of a father, particularly if your father is a believer. God is not a Pastor; God is a Father.

There are fundamental differences in the role that each of these two distinct characters play in the life of a youth. The role of the father is to primarily train his children (male or female) from infancy to adulthood while the Pastor is part of the ministry offices that help to mature believers and help us to get to the point of working together effectively.

The Government: The government has many institutions under it. God's primary intention for the government is clear in the Bible.

> Everyone must submit to governing authorities. For all authority comes from God, and those in positions of authority have been placed there by God. So anyone who rebels against authority is rebelling against what God has instituted, and they will be punished. For the authorities do not strike fear in people who are doing right, but in those who are doing wrong. Would you like to live without fear of the authorities? Do what is right, and they will honor you. The authorities are God's servants, sent for your good. But if you are doing wrong, of course you

> should be afraid, for they have the power to punish you. They are God's servants, sent for the very purpose of punishing those who do what is wrong. So you must submit to them, not only to avoid punishment, but also to keep a clear conscience. Pay your taxes, too, for these same reasons. For government workers need to be paid. They are serving God in what they do. Give to everyone what you owe them: Pay your taxes and government fees to those who collect them, and give respect and honor to those who are in authority. - Romans 13:1-7 NLT

Governments are God's institutions to maintain law and order in every group of people which will include both believers and unbelievers. Without government, there will be chaos and anarchy. Everyone would simply do what seems right in their own opinion - even if it means killing other human beings. God puts the governing laws in place for such people to be under check:

> We know that the law is good when used correctly. For the law was not intended for people who do what is right. It is for people who are lawless and rebellious, who are ungodly and sinful, who consider nothing sacred and defile what is holy, who kill their father or mother or commit other murders.- 1

Timothy 1:8-9 NLT

Training of children is primarily the responsibility of the family, while maintaining law and order in the adult community is the responsibility of Government.

The church is responsible for producing and maturing believers who will be the 'salt of the earth' and who would with God's help, make a difference in their own generations, whether young or old. Hence, a believer's standard of living should be higher than that of the rest of the world because God expects better behavior from us and He has also given us the capacity to perform better than other people. The Bible puts it this way:

> **By his divine power, God has given us everything we need for living a godly life. We have received all of this by coming to know him, the one who called us to himself by means of his marvelous glory and excellence. - 2 Peter1:3 NLT**

Schools were initially family establishments where a number of children were trained together, based on distinct principles that were highly valued by the family. The church developed her own institutions of learning, primarily to teach godly principles as well as ways of making a living. Governments have also established schools to teach their own ideologies such as communism.

Without mincing words, many governments have crossed their God-given boundaries in enacting laws that are clearly counterproductive in the raising of children.

Families have also abandoned their primary responsibilities of raising their own children to schools and churches. Today, we have a large number of confused and selfish youths who know everything about their rights and nothing about their responsibilities. They seem to believe they owe nobody nothing and everybody owes them everything.

Ideally, a child should go to a school that is deliberately picked by his parents for the purpose of preparing them for a career and reinforcing the same values and life principles as also taught by the family.

In a school, a child is encouraged to see other people's perspectives and interact positively with others who do not necessarily have the same point of view or behavior as him or her

A school is not supposed to be the dumping ground for parents who have no time to do what God has called them to do for their own kids. At the end of the day, God is going to judge each person according to the role He expects them to play - which is why I would not put my child in a school that is anti-God!

Chapter 7

THE ROLE OF THE FAMILY IN SETTING UP NEW FAMILIES

Our group of young adults and their parents had a series of interesting discussion on this topic a while ago and I thought it worth sharing in this book.

I had seen many conflicts when it came to the issue of who to marry and when. This is a big challenge, particularly for families that have relocated from their cultural home base.

The questions were, *'Should parents and siblings be involved in my choice of a spouse? How involved should they be? What is the role of culture in the process of choice, courtship and the wedding? What is the role of the church and of the pastor in particular?'*

I will attempt to summarize the discussion which held via Skype during the month of October 2015 to address this issue.

First, we all agreed that it was important that Christian families, irrespective of their cultural backgrounds, be involved with setting up new families based on Biblical principles. Comparing the attitudes of Abraham with that of Isaac on this issue gave insight into some important principles and the outcome of their choices.

Abraham was proactive with the issue of whom Isaac his son would marry. He had relocated from his place of birth according to God's instruction and he knew it was important for Isaac to be married to the right person. He did not leave things to chance, hoping that one day, out of the blues, Isaac would find a suitable wife to marry and they would live happily ever after. He was proactive about this, being conscious of the Word of God concerning him and his descendants.

> **Abraham was now a very old man, and the LORD had blessed him in every way. One day Abraham said to his oldest servant, the man in charge of his household, "Take an oath by putting your hand under my thigh. Swear by the LORD, the God of heaven and earth, that you will not allow my son to marry one of these local Canaanite women. Go instead to my homeland, to my relatives, and find a wife there for my son Isaac." The servant asked, "But what if I can't find a young woman who is willing to travel so far from home? Should I then take Isaac**

> there to live among your relatives in the land you came from?" "No!" Abraham responded. "Be careful never to take my son there. For the LORD, the God of heaven, who took me from my father's house and my native land, solemnly promised to give this land to my descendants. He will send his angel ahead of you, and he will see to it that you find a wife there for my son. If she is unwilling to come back with you, then you are free from this oath of mine. But under no circumstances are you to take my son there. - Genesis 24:1-8 NLT

Isaac on the other hand, was not proactive at all. It took the quarrel between the twin brothers and the bad outcome of Esau's marital decisions to get Jacob to marry differently from Esau. Even at that, both twins ended up as polygamists - whether by choice or by chance - which was not God's original intention for marriage.

> At the age of forty, Esau married two Hittite wives: Judith, the daughter of Beeri, and Basemath, the daughter of Elon. But Esau's wives made life miserable for Isaac and Rebekah. - Genesis 26:34-35 NLT

> "So Isaac called for Jacob, blessed him, and said,

"You must not marry any of these Canaanite women. Instead, go at once to Paddan-aram, to the house of your grandfather Bethuel, and marry one of your uncle Laban's daughters. May God Almighty bless you and give you many children. And may your descendants multiply and become many nations! May God pass on to you and your descendants the blessings he promised to Abraham. May you own this land where you are now living as a foreigner, for God gave this land to Abraham." So Isaac sent Jacob away, and he went to Paddan-aram to stay with his uncle Laban, his mother's brother, the son of Bethuel the Aramean. Esau knew that his father, Isaac, had blessed Jacob and sent him to Paddan-aram to find a wife, and that he had warned Jacob, "You must not marry a Canaanite woman." He also knew that Jacob had obeyed his parents and gone to Paddan-aram. It was now very clear to Esau that his father did not like the local Canaanite women. So Esau visited his uncle Ishmael's family and married one of Ishmael's daughters, in addition to the wives he already had. His new wife's name was Mahalath. She was the sister of Nebaioth and the daughter of Ishmael, Abraham's son. - Genesis 28:1-9 NLT

There are many other examples in the Bible but suffice it to say that the stories of Abraham and Isaac helped us to conclude that family involvement from the onset was important in setting up new families.

Next question is, how involved should the family be?

I will discuss this question based on the perspectives of the young adults in the group. On a general note, marriage is for adults and not for children, so it should not be the responsibility of parents to choose partners for their children or arrange marriages without the direct participation of the two adults who are going to have to live together after the marriage.

The case of Abraham and Isaac was under the Old Testament and though we can learn from the principles demonstrated, we cannot interpret that to mean fathers should look for partners for their sons or daughters. The advice of parents (particularly believers), are nevertheless, invaluable in the whole process.

The perspectives of the young adults

1. Parents should stop comparing their children with other people's children and suggesting the choice of possible partners based on culture e.g. Nigerians vs other cultures.

This was a very interesting discussion. One of the young adults who lived in the UK said she had such a high expectation from Nigerian youths because her parents kept remarking that Nigerian trained youths were much better than the ones around them. She was rather disappointed when she met some Nigerian youths who came to study in the UK but whose conduct and moral values were poor. She concluded that we should be less judgmental based on cultural values. Our best bet is to focus on Biblical rather than cultural standards.

I agree with her wholeheartedly.

2. Parents should instill core values in their children long before they become adults and before the issue of choice of marriage partners arise.

Our second daughter alluded to the fact that she got so used to the injunction that it is not ideal to stay out late at night simply because we kept repeating the Yoruba adage that says "those who were born into good families don't roam about at night". Even as an adult, she still finds it difficult to hang out at night.

They were also taught early enough that there is a difference between a friend and a neighbor and though anyone could be your neighbor, not anyone can be your friend. Friends (male or female) must be carefully chosen and you are better off marrying a friend than a stranger.

3. Parents should answer their children's questions about life in details and not hold back anything. They should talk from their heart and in love.

Many times parents find it embarrassing to talk about sexuality and matters surrounding it. However, they will be shocked to know how much information is available to their very young children. In many schools, children are taught about sexuality from grade four (about eight years of age) and some schools stress the fact that we get to choose whatever gender we want in spite of our biological genders.

Parents should let their children know where they stand on these matters before the schools start teaching them what the parents do not believe in.

One of our young adults said he was told when he got to high school that what happens in school and with school mates stay in that circle and is not meant to be told to parents.

The internet, the television, the recommended novels at school all give so much information that it's hardly possible to keep up pace with them. I wrote a small book *'A letter to My Little Girl'* years ago when my first two daughters were at that stage. This helped me introduce the subject to them and it may help some parents too.

4. Parents should use the framework of disputable and non-disputable matters.

We had discussed what to look for in choosing friends based on the Biblical teachings about disputable and non-disputable matters and that whether we realize it or not, culture plays a big role in the way we judge issues and who we may associate with.

Reading from the book of Romans in the New International Version where that phrase 'disputable matters' was used, we were able to categorize issues into disputable matters and non-disputable matters.

> **Accept the one whose faith is weak, without quarreling over disputable matters. - Romans 14:1 NIV**
>
> **One person's faith allows them to eat anything, but another, whose faith is weak, eats only vegetables. The one who eats everything must not treat with contempt the one who does not, and the one who**

> does not eat everything must not judge the one who does, for God has accepted them." Romans 14:2-3 NIV

> One person considers one day more sacred than another; another considers every day alike. Each of them should be fully convinced in their own mind. Whoever regards one day as special does so to the Lord. Whoever eats meat does so to the Lord, for they give thanks to God; and whoever abstains does so to the Lord and gives thanks to God. - Romans 14:5-6 NIV

> I am convinced, being fully persuaded in the Lord Jesus, that nothing is unclean in itself. But if anyone regards something as unclean, then for that person it is unclean. - Romans 4:14 NIV

There are so many things that we considered 'disputable matters' as long as we are sure an individual is a believer.

What we eat (whether we are vegetarians or not), what we wear (including pants for women, jewelry for men, haircut styles, facial make up, body piercing, tattoos) and when we go to church (Sunday or other days of the week) are all disputable matters.

We are not better or more spiritual if we fall into any of the categories. It would be wise however, to know what each person stands for and WHY. What to look out for primarily are matters of the heart which are clearly stated in the Bible:

> When I wrote to you before, I told you not to associate with people who indulge in sexual sin. But I wasn't talking about unbelievers who indulge in sexual sin, or are greedy, or cheat people, or worship idols. You would have to leave this world to avoid people like that. I meant that you are not to associate with anyone who claims to be a believer yet indulges in sexual sin, or is greedy, or worships idols, or is abusive, or is a drunkard, or cheats people. Don't even eat with such people. - 1 Corinthians 5:9-11 NLT

> These people are grumblers and complainers, living only to satisfy their desires. They brag loudly about themselves, and they flatter others to get what they want. - Jude 1:16 NLT

> Don't you realize that those who do wrong will not inherit the Kingdom of God? Don't fool yourselves. Those who indulge in sexual sin, or who worship idols, or commit adultery, or are male prostitutes, or

> practice homosexuality, or are thieves, or greedy people, or drunkards, or are abusive, or cheat people of these will inherit the Kingdom of God. Some of you were once like that. But you were cleansed; you were made holy; you were made right with God by calling on the name of the Lord Jesus Christ and by the Spirit of our God. - 1 Corinthians 6:9-11 NLT

> In the same way, these people claim authority from their dreams immoral lives, defy authority, and scoff at supernatural beings.   - Jude 1:8 NLT

Smoking, drunkenness and substance abuse fall into the category of those who poison their bodies. Such things dishonor God, the owner of our bodies.

> Don't you realize that your body is the temple of the Holy Spirit, who lives in you and was given to you by God? You do not belong to yourself, for God bought you with a high price. So you must honor God with your body. - 1 Corinthians 6:19-20 NLT

Non disputable matters in setting up new Christian families

1. No marriage to an unbeliever

2. No same sex marriage

3. Divorce is not an option to consider from the onset

4. No living together before marriage. (No Common Law partnership)

5. No marriage with the deliberate intention of not having children, except for specific problems (some believers may disagree with this)

6. No marriage to a carnal Christian

7. No sex before marriage

> For to be carnally minded is death; but to be spiritually minded is life and peace. Because the carnal mind is enmity against God: for it is not subject to the law of God, neither indeed can be. - Romans 8:6-7 KJV

> The mind governed by the flesh is death, but the mind governed by the Spirit is life and peace. The mind governed by the flesh is hostile to God; it does not submit to God's law, nor can it do so. Those who are in the realm of the flesh cannot please God. - Romans 8:6-8 NIV

There are some people who decide not to get married and that is okay, as long as they have the gift of celibacy and they are able to live a life free from sexual immorality.

When the disciples said they would rather not marry because of the high expectations from God about divorce, this was Jesus' response:

> Moses gave you permission to divorce your wives because you are so hard to teach. But it was not like that at the time of creation. I tell you, then, that any man who divorces his wife for any cause other than her unfaithfulness, commits adultery if he marries some other woman." His disciples said to him, "If this is how it is between a man and his wife, it is better not to marry." Jesus answered, "This teaching does not apply to everyone, but only to those to whom God has given it. For there are different reasons why men cannot marry: some, because they were born that way; others, because men made them that way; and others do not marry for the sake of the Kingdom of heaven. Let him who can accept this teaching do so. - Matthew 19:8-12 GNT

Whether or not a believer gets married, he or she comes from a family and has parents and other extended family members. Either way, family still matters and it is wise to follow Biblical guidelines rather than cultural standards which are handed down by traditions from our forefathers. These traditions have not worked in many instances, particularly because of the cultural mixtures we are experiencing in our world today.

I believe that God is demanding better performance from the next generation of marriages and He who began a good work in the lives of our young adults will be faithful to complete it.

Important Things to Decide about Life

- Who to partner with for any venture, most importantly, marriage
- What to do for a living
- How to handle your finances
- Where to live (to start with) and why
- When to start having children
- How many children and how to raise them
- How to relate with extended family
- Which church to go and where to get spiritual nourishment and fellowship

- How to settle disputes and who to go to

- Who to pattern your life after (who mentors you)

Scriptural verses to consider in summary

Dear brothers and sisters, pattern your lives after mine, and learn from those who follow our example. For I have told you often before, and I say it again with tears in my eyes, that there are many whose conduct shows they are really enemies of the cross of Christ. They are headed for destruction. Their god is their appetite, they brag about shameful things, and they think only about this life here on earth. - Philippians 3:17-19 NLT

Then you will not become spiritually dull and indifferent. Instead, you will follow the example of those who are going to inherit God's promises because of their faith and endurance. - Hebrews 6:12 NLT

The sayings of the wise are like the sharp sticks that shepherds use to guide sheep, and collected proverbs are as lasting as firmly driven nails. They have been given by God, the one Shepherd of us all. My child, there is something else to watch out for. There is no end to the writing of books, and too much study will wear you out. After all this, there is only one thing to say: Have reverence for God, and obey his commands, because this is all that we were created for. God is going to judge everything we do, whether good or bad, even things done in secret. - Ecclesiastes 12:11-14 GNT

Let all who are spiritually mature agree on these things. If you disagree on some point, I believe God will make it plain to you. - Philippians 3:15 NLT